W9-AAZ-980

ONCE UPON A TIME
IN VIETNAM

PEARL POETRY PRIZE SERIES

Fluid in Darkness, Frozen in Light • Robert Perchan
Ed Ochester, Judge, 1999

From Sweetness • Debra Marquart
Dorianne Laux, Judge, 2000

Trigger Finger • Micki Myers
Jim Daniels, Judge, 2001

How JFK Killed My Father • Richard M. Berlin
Lisa Glatt, Judge, 2002

Earth's Ends • Andrew Kaufman
Fred Voss, Judge, 2003

The Farmgirl Poems • Elizabeth Oakes
Donna Hilbert, Judge, 2004

This Big Fake World • Ada Limón
Frank X. Gaspar, Judge 2005

Denmark, Kangaroo, Orange • Kevin Griffith
Denise Duhamel, Judge 2006

Through the Glorieta Pass • Lavonne J. Adams
David Hernandez, Judge 2007

See How We Almost Fly • Alison Luterman
Gerald Locklin, Judge 2008

Animal Magnetism • Kim Roberts
Debra Marquart, Judge 2009

JERRY NEREN

Once Upon a Time
in Vietnam

WINNER OF THE
2010
PEARL POETRY PRIZE

Pearl
Editions
LONG BEACH, CALIFORNIA

Library of Congress Control Number: 2011911582

Copyright © 2012 by Jerry Neren
All Rights Reserved
Printed in the United States of America

ISBN 978-1-888219-40-1

The poems in this book are products of the author's imagination. Names, characters, and incidents are fictional and any resemblance to actual persons, living or dead, or any relationship to actual events, locales, and institutions, is entirely coincidental.

Book design & cover illustration by Marilyn Johnson

This publisher is a proud member of

[clmp]

COUNCIL OF LITERARY MAGAZINES & PRESSES
w w w . c l m p . o r g

PEARL EDITIONS
3030 E. Second Street
Long Beach, California 90803

www.pearlmag.com

*This book is dedicated to those who suffered seen
and unseen wounds.*

CONTENTS

PREFACE

A S CLEARLY AS BEETHOVEN could attribute his inspiration for composing the *Pastoral Symphony* to regular walks in the countryside around Vienna; as clearly as Gershwin could attribute his inspiration for composing the symphonic tone poem, *An American in Paris*, to the time spent in the French capital in the 1920s; as unmistakably, even through the blur of years, can I ascribe my inspiration for writing *Once Upon a Time in Vietnam*, a narrative in verse, to someone I once saw—a man who was wearing a jacket, a jacket nondescript in every sense of the word, except for the country of Vietnam embroidered on the back; except for the words inscribed beneath:

> When I die
> I'm going to heaven
> because I've already been to hell.

Because of that chance encounter, I set about to write what I imagined was the "hell" he'd been through; and what I imagined, over the course of the more than twenty years it took to complete the work, was a mental hell.

The story tracks a young man from the time he is drafted into the army right out of college; suffers a complete mental breakdown during his tour of combat duty; continues to struggle with his mental wound upon his return home; and, finally, finds a way to reconstruct his demolished life, which brings him some degree of peace and resolution in light of everything he experienced during the war, including the role he played in the death and destruction that took place in Vietnam.

The landscape of the poems is entirely interior—an inner world of mental anguish; the mental anguish of combatants in a war zone where stress casualties can run as high as battle casualties; the mental anguish of a million men and women who served in Vietnam, and consequently, suffered from the psychological wound of Post-Traumatic Stress Disorder. Prior to Vietnam, "irritable heart" in the Civil War, "shell shock" in World

War I, and "battle fatigue" in World War II, were terms used to describe what the American Psychiatric Association codified in 1980 as Post-Traumatic Stress Disorder, allowing patients to receive needed treatment. Regardless of what this mental hell is called, or wasn't called back in the Stone Age when people were beating each other to a fare-thee-well with clubs, one thing can be said for sure: no one has ever come home from war unchanged.

In 1788, Alexander Hamilton wrote in *The Federalist*: "To judge from the history of mankind, we shall be compelled to conclude that the fiery and destructive passions of war reign in the human breast with much more powerful sway than the mild and beneficent sentiments of peace . . ." And for that reason, this book is written with the hope that all of us, that all the nations of the world, will someday prove him wrong.

—Jerry Neren

Once Upon a Time
in Vietnam

*War is a conflict that doesn't determine who is right
or who is wrong but who is left.*

—Anonymous

Prologue

BOOT CAMP

Fort Benning, Georgia

Five weeks left of boot camp
and Sergeant Krulak caws:
Owr yoo-nit's shippin' owt
'n naahn-dee daiize t' Vee-et-naahm—
and stories spread like flu
about a place

that most of us couldn't even locate on a map;
about the torture the North Vietnamese
mete out on POWs;
about the soldiers poisoned by Agent Orange,
their insides devoured like plankton by a whale;
about the infantryman

who triggered a land mine rated at
·three-hundred pounds of TNT,
the crater it created as commodious
as a double bungalow,
his body blown into as many bits
as packages on Santa's sleigh;

about GIs
combing the countryside
on search-and-destroy operations,
seeking an enemy
elusive as a mirage—
humans hunting humans

with AK-47s and M-16s
and claymores and bangalores
and napalm and pocket bombs
and mortars and rockets
and hand grenades and booby traps
and spider holes and Zippo raids—

humans hunting humans
and I can't even harm a fly,
and I was a concert pianist
before I was drafted;
and as the days drop off the calendar
like feathers from a dying bird,

fear grows inside of me
like mushrooms in a cave,
and I cannot eat,
and I cannot sleep,
and many a night I even weep
into my pillow secretly

and I haven't even left Georgia yet.

PART ONE:

The Battle Front

THE KILLING LINE

1.

Propped on pillows in the psych ward
of a veterans hospital,
I watch the television documentary

Vietnam: Ten Years After the Fall of Saigon

and I think back
to my second week in Vietnam
when B Troop clashed with
a Viet Cong guerrilla unit
near the DMZ.
In the midst of the fray I recalled

those sunny Sunday afternoons
when I
and friends of mine
would bike up to the park on top
of St. Clair Hill.
For us, that wooded park became
a battlefield:
our rifles and bayonets,
long sticks;
our hand grenades,
small stones;
our voices mimicking
explosions and gunfire.
Any Sunday I'd be killed
a dozen times at least;
and each time I'd be killed,

I'd perform a death scene
worthy of an Oscar.
Moments later, as if resurrected,
I'd bounce back up,
despite the enemy's admonishments,
rejoin the melee
only to be killed
and killed again.
At five o'clock,
I'd brush myself off
and bike back home,
wash up,
sit down to dinner.

During that firefight near the DMZ,
I learned:
when someone is killed, there is
no getting up,
no brushing off,
no biking home.

2.

The tropic sun,
like something set ablaze
with napalm,
was setting over the Saigon River
when Eddie strolled back into camp,
returning from another
killing spree.
Eddie didn't hate the North Vietnamese.
In fact, his killing sprees
had nothing whatsoever to do

with Vietnam.
Eddie would have spreed
in New York City, Colorado
Springs or Minneapolis.
Pure coincidence
his flings
so happened to be in Nam.
Yet none of us thought Eddie odd:
each of us had killed;
Eddie just did more of it.
Besides, Sadowski said,
in a system of free enterprise,
it is commendable, is it not,
when someone shows some initiative.

Unlike his other romps,
Eddie came back this time
wearing a necklace made
of human ears.
Peewee, like the rest of us,
knew how good at killing Eddie was.
But Peewee said he never dreamed
that Eddie had another side,
that Eddie had a flair
for arts and crafts.
Chompy kept eating
a C-rations can of pears;
Yo-Yo kept plunking "Little Darling"
on his ukulele;
Lucky kept playing solitaire,
slipping a queen beneath a king;
Justice kept waxing

his handle-bar mustachio;
others
simply shrugged,
as if to say,
boys will be boys.
Though no one knew it at the time,
I went insane.

3.

I saw men go mad
in Vietnam.
I saw Rosey try to swallow
a live grenade.
All we could do was
hit the ground,
cover up.
I saw Goldfarb laugh
when Buster, his buddy,
triggered a land mine,
got blown to bits.
I saw Mankiewicz
open up on us
with his machine gun.
By the time that Sergeant Krulak
flattened him with his forty-five,
Mankiewicz had killed
three and wounded eight.
I saw Olsen playing
checkers with Moses.
I saw screamers and babblers.
I saw weepers.
I was a smiler.

4.

Because of the range of reactions
to Eddie's necklace,
no one thought unusual
my smiling,
until next morning,
until they found me sitting
in the exact same attitude,
on the exact same crate of mortar shells
still smiling.
It was then they realized
it wasn't Eddie I was smiling at;
realized
that I'd laid down
my M-16 rifle and bayonet,
my hand grenades and ammo belt,
walked off the killing line.
It was then they realized
I'd left them, left
that fungal fairyland
of Vietnam,
gone
to some happier,
some saner place.

CASE HISTORY I

*From a presentation at the Twenty-seventh
International Psychiatric Congress
Oslo, Norway*

Eugene was born in St. Paul, Minnesota, where he grew up a jovial, sociable, active child of high intelligence. None of his grandparents, nor his parents, ever showed signs of mental disorder. Nor did Eugene have any previous history of mental illness, and seemed in every regard, prior to his breakdown in Vietnam, a happy, normal, well-adjusted young man.

Eugene and Dominick—the patient's friend since childhood—received their graduate degrees in music from the University of Minnesota. Both showed promising classical careers: the patient as a pianist; his friend as a tenor, having finished first in a regional audition sponsored by the Metropolitan Opera—the patient his piano accompanist. Their student deferments from military service at an end, the patient and his friend were drafted into the army.

As the patient's tour of duty in Vietnam wore on, certain combat stresses, not atypical of those experienced in an active war theater, started undermining his morale and his emotional stability. First and foremost was the loss of Dominick, his lifelong friend, upon whom he was greatly dependent and who was a source of strength to him. This trauma caused the patient untold amounts of pain and guilt, and he constantly blamed himself for his friend's death even though he was not in the least negligent. He carried on with grim determination but, as more and more of his comrades were lost; as he became obsessed with thoughts of home and peace; as he became increasingly concerned for his own personal welfare and safety; and when he witnessed atrocities perpetrated by the Viet Cong as well as by fellow soldiers, he finally broke down.

Eugene's psychosis was the catatonic variety of schizophrenia, the central features of which were stupor and mutism. He sat in one position; his saliva was not swallowed so that it accumulated and fell from his mouth; he had to be dressed and undressed; he had to be moved in bed; he had to be fed primarily through a tube; and he never spoke. Every modality of treatment known to modern psychiatry for treating his particular disorder, including insulin shock therapy, electroshock therapy, psychotherapy, and psychotropic drugs, was attempted, but failing all, we simply let him be. And even when his parents and his fiancée would visit him, he never once knew who they were, and never said a single word.

As in a magic sleep, time passed without his knowing it. And then one day, he suddenly awoke, oblivious to the enormous span of time that had elapsed, a span of time that was to him but as a moment—woke up in a fright and asked the nurse to tell him where he was, for he woke up to find that he was not in Vietnam, as he supposed, but in a veterans hospital; woke up to find the war in Vietnam had ended; woke up to find his parents dead, his fiancée married to another man; woke up to find that he was forty-one not twenty-four.

OPEN YOUR EYES A LITTLE

Were it not for the high stone walls
and guarded gate,
I'd think this some lovely park
instead of a place for mincemeat minds,
I muse while sitting outside this summer morning,
watching the thirsty sun
lap up what few drops remain of milky haze,
watching the ducks and geese
skimming over the surface of the pond
like string-drawn toys on wheels,

a cup of coffee,
a small cigar,
the transistor radio playing Mozart's opera
Le Nozze di Figaro
and how I laugh
as once again I see you
perched like some great bird
on top a blasted stump of tree
singing arias; singing arias
that resonated through

the jungles of Vietnam,
that place we called "the real surreal,"
that place you said it would have been your luck
to win a trip to.
And then you confided:
instead of pursuing a career
with the Metropolitan Opera,
that you would prefer to concert tour
with me, yes, I would be
your piano accompanist.

But how a thing like war
can change things, Dominick.
Inside this veterans hospital
I have much time to think.
And now if you were to say,
"Eugene, come, our country goes to war,"
I would tell you,
"Dominick, as you can see,
I have geraniums I must replant."
Or if you were to say,

"Eugene, come, we are in need of recreation;
let's go up north,
fish and hunt and make a time of it,"
I would tell you,
"Dom, Dom, my friend,
each time I'd see those fishes
strung on stringers,
I'd see our boys
hung from trees like Christmas ornaments;
each time I'd hear the wounded cries of the raccoons,

I'd hear the village children."
And at the oddest times,
most often in the full, bright sun
I see a deer,
a deer with an arrow
out both sides his neck.
And each time I see
the puddles of blood he leaves behind
with prints of hooves beside them,
each time I find him

on knees and hocks
nose down in his blood,
each time I hear
the bubbling of his breath in his blood,
each time I watch him die,
I see you again.
Forgive me, Dominick,
it is not like me
to carry on like this.
You must think I've laced

my cup of coffee,
or that this small cigar
is homemade blend.
Listen! Listen!
They near the end of *Figaro*
and how they play and how he sings
your favorite aria:
Aprite un po' quegl' occhi.
Ah, what music, what music
we could have made.

Great Poem ✗

SURVIVAL MANUAL FOR VIETNAM

I. INTRODUCTION

A. In order to physically survive
   inside a combat zone,
   just follow one simple rule:
   do not get killed.

B. In order to mentally survive
   inside a combat zone,
   you need to follow three,
   not quite as simple, rules
   neither thumb-tacked
   to your barracks' bulletin board,
   nor found *italicized*
   in the army rules and regs,
   nor presented in chalk talks
   in boot camp training rooms,
   nor parceled out
   by your commanding officer
   for you to read
   and memorize
   and then destroy
   prior to landing in Da Nang,
   for these are unspoken and unwritten rules
   you would have had to learn
   the way a child learns not
   to touch a flame
   but only after first touching it
   if not for this manual.

To the extent you keep these rules,
the good news is
you'll make it through your twelve-month tour
of combat duty in Vietnam,
and you'll go home,
a little worse, of course, for wear,
but you'll go home.

To the extent you break these rules,
the bad news is
the following formula will then apply:
break one,
and you will have nightmares of Vietnam
for the rest of your life;
break two,
and you will wander
homeless through the days and through the nights
of city streets;
break three,
and you will still go home,
but with your mind inside
a body bag.

II. RULE NUMBER ONE

Be friendly, and all of that,
but never get too close
to anyone in your platoon,
for this is not Hometown, U.S.A.
where friends will be around
as long as the oak tree in your yard,
but Vietnam
where in a combat zone
like Khe Sanh or Tien Phu
however many friends you'll make
will more than likely be
as many friends as you
in just a few
short weeks
or days
or even in just a finger snap
will lose
and neither from natural causes,
nor illness, nor disease,
but suddenly
and violently
and sometimes while even in
your young trembling and unbelieving arms.
So never ever become fast friends
with anyone in your platoon,
for if you do,
what happened to

Rosey,
    when Artie, wrapped
    inside a poncho like a Slim Jim in cellophane,
    sloshed up to him in driving rain
    and said in that surprisingly high-pitched voice
    for someone who weighed two-sixty-five,
    Can you believe,
    I mean, can you believe,
    your pal, Spumoni, just took a tracer round
    right in the mouth,
    I mean, right in the mouth,
    blew off the back of his head
    but never even touched
    his lips or his teeth
    when it went in.
    He must've been yakking at the time,
    or laughing at a joke,
    or maybe yawning even,
    when it went in,
    I mean, it's like he breathed it in
    just like a goddamned gnat.
    Rosey's face
    grew gray as that monsoonal day.
    And calm as a midnight street,
    Rosey unclipped from his webbed belt
    a hand grenade
    and twisted it into his mouth
    and pulled the pin,
    and what could Artie do except
    hit the ground, cover up—

or to Mad Max,
    when his buddy, Alphabet,
    got caught in an enemy cross-fire.
    Alphabet was bleeding
    from so many AK-47 bullet holes,
    it looked as if he were crushed between
    two beds of nails.
    Mad Max was holding him
    as tightly as a tourniquet
    as if by so doing he could stop
    the bleeding from all those holes.
    And no one could separate
    Mad Max from Alphabet,
    not even after Alphabet was dead.
    And even when the medevac touched down,
    the medics had to load them both
    into the chopper
    still locked together like
    two lovers in
    some sort of strange, slow dance—

or to the Fonz,
    when Estevez, his confidant,
    while waltzing over to
    a stand of banyans to take a pee,
    triggered a land mine rated at
    two-hundred pounds of TNT.
    What little was left of Estevez
    was not enough to fill
    a baggie, let alone
    a body bag.

On hands and knees, the Fonz
collected whatever odds
and ends that he could find
and tried to fit them
like the pieces of a jigsaw puzzle
into what once was Estevez—

will happen, and you can take this to the bank,
to you.

III. Rule Number Two

As men who butcher in a slaughterhouse
must distance themselves
from the cows and the pigs
by deeming them dumb and doltish beasts
that neither have feet but hooves,
nor skin but hide,
nor weep but stare,
nor dine but graze,
nor circles of friends but herds,
nor make deep and adoring love
but mount and mate,
if they are to lift that sledge
and crush that skull,
if they are to run that knife
across that throat,
so you must learn as well
to distance yourself from those
whom you must kill.
Following are three suggested ways
of distancing yourself,
ways which will make it easier,
if not enjoyable,
for you to kill:

(1) Dehumanize

While lobbing a hand grenade
or tossing a satchel charge
into a tunnel or a cave,
imagine the enemy
as creepy and crawly

as rats
and roaches that
the U.S. Government is paying you to
exterminate.

(2) Politicize

On muggy mornings when marching off
on search-and-destroy operations,
remember that just as someone has to kill
if we're to have our Big Macs and KFC,
so you must kill
if we are to have democracy.

(3) Philosophize

Each time you torch
Vietnamese villages
with suspected Viet Cong,
follow the logical, not the moral, school
of thought professing that in a war, the more
of them you kill—
in fact, the more the merrier—
the greater will be the chance
that you will win,
the greater will be the chance
that you will survive.

Be mindful, then, of rule number two
by dissociating yourself from those
whom you must kill,
and never embrace the sentiment
that they, like you, have thoughts
of home and family

while hunkered down in bunkers in
the fright of night;
that they, like you, have hobbies and interests
like stamp collecting and gardening;
that they, like you, have companion dogs
they like to take on strolls;
that they, like you, have messengers
who walk up those unpaved paths
to thatch huts with dirt floors
and knock on bamboo doors
and say,
not in English but Vietnamese,
I'm sorry, but your son, your son—

for if you do,
to even think of killing them would be
like killing your own,
and if you think like this,
then you won't want to kill them anymore,
and when you don't,
you'll run the risk
that they will kill you instead,
or that the army will kill you for
not killing them,
and this creates
a conflict that you can't resolve—
a paralytic inability to choose between
your life and theirs,
and one way to resolve
an irresolvable conflict is
to go insane.

IV. Rule Number Three

Never question
why you're in Vietnam,
and always deep-down inside believe
those starry generals in Arlington
and those high-ups in Washington
would never send
a couple million adolescent men
to hell
if not for reasons
sane,
if not for reasons
sound,
even though you're the one who's there,
who's on the killing line
in Vietnam,
while they are here,
not on the killing line
inside the Pentagon,
not on the killing line
inside the Oval Office in Washington;

and always deep-down inside believe
you wouldn't be there were it not
in the best interests of
the South Vietnamese,
even though the people
you're there supposedly to help
neither shower you with flowers,
nor with kisses,
the way the Europeans did
GIs in World War II,
but spit on you

Saviors of the world

and catcall epithets instead
like doo-mommies while you're marching through
their thatch and bamboo villages
and shout at you to go home
and let them farm in peace
their rice paddies and their fields of tea;

and always deep-down inside believe
that you are the saviors of the world,
even though such notions,
romantic as they may be, don't mean
a fat rat's ass
to eighteen- and nineteen-year-old kids
whose only thoughts
are sex inside
the Hung Dao Hotel
on Tu Do Street, Saigon,
or getting drunk,
or getting stoned,
or wasting gooks,
for these are the only ways
to vent your anger, vent
your hate
and your frustrations in the Nam;

and always deep-down inside believe
that getting paid
a couple hundred bucks a month
and all the Viet Cong you can kill,
and all the C-rations you can eat,
and all the jungle rot you can treat,
and all the body bags you can fill,
and all the "Dear John" letters you can read,
and all the monsoon muck you can slog,

27

and all the clotted traches you can unclog,
and all the leeches you can feed,
is a pretty sweet deal.

So never question why you're in Vietnam,
for if you do,
you won't come up with one good reason why,
and when you can't,
then you won't want to be there anymore,
and when you don't,
then you'll create
some sort of mental game
to take your mind off things,
like thinking of the time—
that summertime
when just a boy of ten—
you lived inside a tree house that you built,
and then you'll think about it once a week,
and then you'll think about it once a day,
then all the time,
then pretty soon

you'll *be* that boy of ten again,
and you will *be* inside that tree house
living happily the summer long,
and no one and nothing—
neither your first sergeant, nor
the medics, nor the chaplain, nor
psychiatrists, nor Thorazine,
nor megavolts of electroshock therapy
enough to dim the hospital's lights,
nor pleas of parents,
nor even those of your fiancée—
will ever get you down from there.

THE STUFF OF WHICH DREAMS ARE MADE

A freighterful of different things
could make a man go mad
in Vietnam,
and one of them was fear,
a constant-as-a-toothache kind of fear
of getting killed,
or not getting killed
and going home
without arms like a stool,

or getting captured by
the North Vietnamese because
we knew
the kinds of things that they would do.
Another one
was way too much of certain things
like jungle,
triple- and quadruple-canopy jungle,
week after week after week;

like pining every minute of the day
for the girl you left
behind in Boise, Idaho
and how you loved
to simply gaze at her
because her nose had the cutest way
of twitching like a rabbit's when she talked;
like on and on and on envisioning
those Sunday morning breakfasts

29

of fried salami and scrambled eggs
and buttered chunks
of homemade cheese-and-onion bread
and fresh-squeezed orange juice with
the pulp in it
your mom would make for you;
and even way too much
of something as simple as a word,
as the sound of a word

like Vietnam—
which neither has
the soft and sensuous sound of France,
nor the dreamy sound of Switzerland,
nor the mysterious-sounding sound
of Ecuador
or Israel
or even Africa,
but has a kind of flinty edge,

a sort of scary stridency—
could make a man go
loony tunes and merry melodies,
especially if he thought about that word too much,
especially if he said that word out loud,
and I mean really loud,
umpteen times a day,
day after day,
like Bernie did.

And so the story's this:
it wasn't any one of these,
nor even anything of the sort,
but Eddie who was the fall guy for
my going insane,
although, in truth, the fault
was mine and mine alone,
for how could anyone have known,
unless I chose to share the fact,

which I did not,
that I had been breaking all
three rules for months
when they were neither spoken nor written rules
that anyone could see or hear
if you were violating, or
if you were not,
like cleaning and oiling your M-16,
or spraying with fungicide

your feet each day,
or addressing as, sir, an officer,
or keeping while on night patrol
as silent as a stump.
And so the story's this:
when Eddie strolled back into camp,
returning from another
killing spree,
I was already as tottery as a tree

Ham & lima beans

sawn nearly through,
needing just one more thing
of anything at all—
another crappy cup of coffee,
another cold C-rations can
of ham and lima beans,
another tasteless joke,
another incoming mortar shell,
another outgoing mortar shell,

another day without a bath,
another body bag,
another day of sun,
another day of rain—
to topple me.
And so the story's this:
it wasn't any one of these,
nor Eddie even,
but a dream that turned out

to be the straw,
a dream I began to dream
the moment I compromised
those three uncompromising rules—
this one recurring dream,
a dream so terrible
that after a couple months of dreaming it
I could not bear to sleep
for fear of dreaming it again.

And so the story's this:
when Eddie strolled back into camp,
wearing a necklace made
of human ears,
it's true I went insane,
but not because
of Eddie, but
because I hadn't slept
in five straight days.

THE DREAM

I dreamed I was still in Vietnam,
dreamed I was driving
a locomotive
the size of a ten-story building
pulling a thousand miles
of hearses coupled each
to each like railway cars.
Inside each hearse,
a coffin made of pine.
Inside the coffins
were American servicemen
as well as Viet Cong
and North Vietnamese;

inside were young and old village women;
inside were young and old village men;
inside were children;
inside were chickens and water buffalo;
inside were goats and dogs and pigs;
inside a coffin two-inches square,
a butterfly,
a yellow butterfly.
The landscape
as barren as salt flats
except for trees,
trees bordering the tracks,
trees leafless and lifeless from defoliants;

except for birds,
birds queuing the branches,
as if all the birds in the world
had congregated there—
all those birds
and not a one
was singing,
all those birds
and every one
was silent.
The tracks came to an end inside
a cemetery
vast as Vietnam itself.

I looked around
and there
was no one there,
just me
and all those hearses,
a thousand miles of hearses;
just me
and all those coffins,
a thousand miles of coffins;
and there
was no one there
to bury them,
to say the eulogies,

just me.

To Kill a Man

War is insane
and its insanity is so virulent
that you can catch it as easily
as you catch a cold.

—Anthony Hecht
Essays on War 1951

Three weeks in Vietnam
and our patrol
is searching for any signs of enemy
along a communist infiltration route
in War Zone C
near the Cambodian border.
The heat as unrelenting as if the earth itself
were stricken with blackwater fever,
the air as hazy as a smoke-filled bar,
and dusk is wrapping itself around us like
a jungle snake
when, fifty or sixty feet ahead,
just off the trail,
a bivouac of Viet Cong.
Lieutenant Kravitz runs
a finger across his throat
which means
to kill them quickly,
then presses a finger vertically against his lips
which means
to kill them quietly
using our field knives or
our bayonets.

And it was then—
the moment we converged upon
then rushed their encampment;
the moment that I saw
the pleading and terror
on his young face;
the moment that I thrust
my bayonet into his chest
impaling him
like a fish on a spear;
the moment I extracted the bayonet
and watched his face turn pale as ice;
the moment he collapsed
in a heap at my feet,
his arms around my legs;
the moment I softly said
to no one in particular,
What have I done?—
yes, it was then,
inside my mind,
the virus of war's insanity
began to incubate.

FROM HERE TO THERE

To walk around fifty feet
from here, a combat outpost near Binh Dinh,
to there, the edge of a mangrove swamp,
to simply take a pee,
is not the kind of thing
you'd ordinarily think about,
say, if you worked inside
an office building in downtown Minneapolis,
or even in your own home in Omaha,
but this was Vietnam
and nothing was ordinary here,
and so I thought about it
step after step after step,
heart pounding, palms sweating
with each step I took—
like Russian roulette,
each step
a spinning of the cylinder,
a pulling of the trigger,
spin
and pull,
spin
and pull,
each step
for fifty steps,
never knowing which step
might be the one
to trigger a booby-trapped artillery round
camouflaged by some Viet Cong
that blows me to kingdom come
in so many pieces that
not even the great, all-knowing God
could say for certain who I was.

To Win a War

Winning isn't everything.
Winning is the only thing.
　　　　—Vince Lombardi

It wasn't top secret
that we were sent to Vietnam
to do the only thing we were trained to do,
which was to kill,

and so we killed—

partly because of incentives—
like added leave time
in Da Nang and Saigon,
and cases of Munich beer,
and cartons of Turkish cigarettes,
and prostitutes
who always brought opium—
for meeting or
exceeding our quota of kills;

and killed—

everyone in sight,
for unlike other wars
in which the good guys wore
one kind of uniform,
the bad guys another kind,
so that you always knew
exactly who
to kill,

the Nam was a guerrilla war
where anyone—
old village men
and women, even children, too—
could be
the enemy;

and killed—

everything in sight,
like pigs and goats
and chickens and water buffalo,
but not because we thought them enemy,
but out of anger,
out of frustration not knowing who
was enemy
and who was not,
and not knowing why
in hell we were in Nam;

and killed—

with Agent Orange,
the military code name for
the devilish defoliant
we sprayed in Laos and
South Vietnam
over jungles and over farms
(and sometimes over our own men)
so as to kill the shrubs
and kill the trees

where enemy
would snipe at us;
so as to kill the grazing lands
which kills, of course, the animals
that need to graze;
so as to kill the food crops
such as rice and maize
and sweet potatoes and sugar cane
which kills, of course, the villagers
who need to eat;

and killed—

but mainly because
from personal experience
we knew
that when you kill a man,
his comrades'
hearts
and sometimes
minds
will follow.

Hearts & minds

CASE HISTORY II

*From a presentation at the Twenty-ninth
International Psychiatric Congress
London, England*

Seventeen years to the day that Eugene went insane in Vietnam, he suddenly awoke from his psychotic state, as if just prior to his going insane, he set some sort of internal alarm clock to awaken him after exactly seventeen years had elapsed.

At the root of Eugene's psychosis was a conflict that he was powerless to resolve, which was, that a totally non-violent young man was taught, then made to kill. Compounding this conflict was his growing estrangement from, and heightening cynicism towards, a world that still believed in war. And neither electing suicide, nor wishing to desert and be branded as a coward or labeled as a quitter, he really had no alternative but to go insane, and when he did, he set an internal clock to awaken him seventeen years later to the day.

For all those years, Eugene lay dormant as the seed of a desert poppy when confronted with the harsh reality of drought. Because the absence of rain is beyond its power to resolve, the seed adapts by withdrawing into a safe, protective and impenetrable cocoon, letting time and time alone resolve what it cannot. The seed will lie dormant for ten or more years, waiting and hoping for the rain that will burst it into bloom. Similarly, Eugene withdrew into the cocoon of insanity, waiting and hoping for that which time and only time alone could bring to pass—for his equivalent of rain that would coax him out of his cocoon, but only after seventeen years had passed.

Above and beyond the situational element of conflict, and the attitudinal elements of estrangement and cynicism that contributed to his schizophrenic condition, Eugene's withdrawal into a state of total sensory deprivation was a mental hunger strike intended to protest war in general, and, in particular, the war in Vietnam; and it was also a mental hair shirt intended as self-punishment and penance for the part he played in the death and the destruction in Vietnam, similar to Henchard in Thomas Hardy's *The Mayor of Casterbridge* who vowed sobriety for twenty-one years as both self-punishment as well as penance for the sin of selling his wife at a county fair while he was drunk.

As can be seen, in order for us to try to understand this highly complex and unusual case, we had to take into consideration factors other than psychological, such as ethics, morals, philosophy, religion and even literature for Eugene's withdrawing into the stupor and mutism of catatonic schizophrenia, for Eugene was a highly moral, principled and deeply devout, as well as a happy and well-adjusted young man who would have never gone insane had he never gone to Vietnam. Or, put another way, just as a chameleon takes on the color of its immediate environment, Eugene took on the color of Vietnam: the color of insanity.

Seventeen years to the day that Eugene went insane in Vietnam, he suddenly awoke—time enough, he must have thought, for the war to end; time enough, he must have felt, for himself to heal; time enough, he must have hoped, for the world to change.

LAST WEEKEND

Saturday and I don't mind
that it is raining out,
don't mind that I am forty-four,
and I don't even mind
the hospital today,
for this is my last weekend here.
Packing my belongings, I come across
a clipping from the Sunday St. Paul Pioneer Press:
    ST. PAULITE WINS THE REGIONAL
    METROPOLITAN OPERA AUDITION

I think back twenty years,
back to the final night
of competition at Northrop Auditorium,
and I was seated at a Steinway concert grand,
and Dominick was singing the aria
O monumento
from Ponchielli's La Gioconda
and I could not remember
his voice ever lovelier.
And how can I forget that next day, Sunday,

when Dominick and I
packed with pepper Brie
and little loaves of sourdough bread
a wicker picnic basket,
filled with sparkling Burgundy
a Coca-Cola cooler,
drove in Dom's old 1950 Chevy
to Hidden Falls and celebrated,
pretending not to see
each other's sadness,

for we would be leaving soon for Vietnam.
And how can I forget that Friday,
ten months later,
sun high overhead,
rice paddies everywhere,
our squad, two miles
from the Cambodian border,
was setting up an ambush,
when Dom went down,
an arrow out both sides his neck,

a booby trap that either he or I set off,
a trap rigged by some Viet Cong guerrilla,
and I was holding him,
yes, I remember holding him.
It is raining harder now,
and I am leaving Monday,
and I am returning to St. Paul,
find some place to live,
some sort of work to do,
and there'll be no one waiting.

PART TWO:

The Home Front

FIRST WEEKEND

*after the
way*

I knew it was going to be
one of those days
the moment I woke up this morning
and found myself covered by
a morgue sheet of depression;
daylight barging into the bedroom,
barging into my eyes
that slit themselves like Venetian blinds
to ward off the warlike intrusion;
nor could I have even said with certainty

how long I had been supine
since my clock radio went off,
except to say that when it did, it exploded with
Tchaikovsky's *1812 Overture,*
then something else after that
I could not for the life of me recognize,
maybe Wagner, maybe Schönberg,
didn't know, didn't care;
and, by and by, when I
tried getting out of bed,

I felt as though I weighed a thousand pounds,
as if earth's gravitational force had gone berserk.
And now it's early Saturday afternoon,
and I am still in pajamas and a robe,
and this is my first weekend home,
and I am sitting in a hard-backed chair,
and I am looking out
the open window in my room
on the top floor of
a rickety rooming house

in St. Paul's old West Side,
and I am drinking a six-ounce can of V-8 juice,
and I am listening to
the day after day of rain,
and I am listening as well
to the Saturday afternoon opera
on public radio
as Luciano Pavarotti and Beverly Sills
are singing the love duet
Addio, o dolce svegliare

from Puccini's *La Bohéme*,
and Monday I start working as a day laborer
in a warehouse or factory—
two days between now and then,
alone and by myself,
to think
how I am suddenly forty-four
with as much to look forward to
as a butterfly pinned in some collector's book;
how Vietnam

gobbled my whole life whole
like a hognose snake a toad;
how I would give anything
if I could be somewhere, anywhere right now
where people are,
say, even a Laundromat,
where people are washing and drying clothes
and telling stories and telling jokes
and smoking Winston and Salem cigarettes
and drinking Cokes and Mountain Dews

50

and eating Fritos and salted nut rolls vended from
a bank of machines that sits
along a faded and paint-chipped wall,
or even inside a movie house
where people are fugitives
for a couple of hours
from the prisons of their lives,
and where I wouldn't even mind
if sitting next to me were someone who
is munching on popcorn and slurping some soda,

for I would find comforting
that sound,
find comforting any kind
of human sound.
And as the rain rains on,
it having rained so many days now in a row
that all of God's creatures must be wondering
if there was ever
even such a thing as sun;
and as the daylight dims into

late afternoon,
then darkens into dusk
which deepens, cloaking everything
in the habit of a nun,
I look beyond the rooming house,
beyond the Tom Thumb Superette
which sits on a corner catty-corner from
Kowalski's Wine & Liquor Store,
beyond the bustling Burger King,
beyond the languishing Long John Silver Fish 'n' Chips,

beyond the high-density-housing construction site
where stands a crane
that looks for all the world
like some colossal gallows of the sort
for hanging giants,
beyond the lights of houses
filled with families
now readying for bed,
the children dillydallying,
the parents—but now my thoughts,

like a faithful dog that has wandered off,
find their way back to the rooming house,
where all day long I've imagined that
my telephone begins to ring,
imagine that someone who remembers me,
heard I was back,
is calling to say hello,
to say they're sorry about the war
and all that I've been through,
to say let's get together soon,

or maybe it's even someone who
has dialed my number by mistake,
and I imagine not answering
for half-a-dozen rings or so,
and when I do, I answer breathlessly
and a little annoyed,
as if I were otherwise engaged
with someone or something much more important than
the everyday ringing of a phone.
And just as Puccini's *La Boheme* gave way

to Chopin's Heroic Polonaise,
and Chopin gave way to Bruckner's Seventh Symphony,
and Bruckner gave way to Saint-Saëns' Fourth
Piano Concerto, Saint-Saëns gives way
to Chic Corea and Woody Herman
as the Saturday all-night jazz show comes on the air,
and now it's the music of Michel Legrand,
his score for the film
The Umbrellas of Cherbourg
and Ella Fitzgerald is singing the theme song

"If It Takes Forever I Will Wait for You"
the same as she sang it with
the Oscar Peterson Trio twenty years ago
at Freddie's, a nightclub
in downtown Minneapolis,
and it was a Saturday,
and it was late evening,
and it was raining cats and dogs,
and Bethany and I
were seated at a small corner table garnished with

a lit candle and a pink peony in
a slender, cut-glass vase,
and the air was hazy with the smoke
of cigarettes that seemed
as romantic as fog,
and the air was seasoned with the smell
of beer-cheese soup
and anchovies on garlic-buttered toast
and porterhouse steak and lobster thermidor
with a side of potatoes au gratin

served sizzling on red-hot trays with asbestos mitts,
and everyone in Freddie's seemed so in love,
and we were so in love,
and tears were in your eyes
when, over our after-dinner drink of anisette,
I gave you an engagement ring,
and tears were in your eyes,
for this was to be our last
weekend together before I left
for Vietnam,

and just as Ella was singing, I will wait for you,
you whispered, in unison with her,
those very same words to me;
and whispered those words again that night
on my lips on my ears on my chest
at your apartment on Marshall Avenue;
and again and again,
on Monday morning just before
I boarded the U.S. Army troop transport plane,
you whispered those words to me;

and I was using those words like battle gear
to fight off the darkness
the day I was in the twelfth month of my tour
with less than two weeks left,
the day I was sitting on a crate of mortar shells
inside a campsite inside a combat zone
along the Saigon River,
and I remember looking down
and there on the ground in front of me
I saw myself

in thousands of tiny shards,
as if I were made of glass
and just got hit by an artillery shell.
And now the sound
of Bach's B-minor Mass
announces that it is 6:00 a.m.
and that the all-night jazz show has given way
to classical music once again
as Saturday has given way to Sunday
and dark has given way to dawn,

and I am still sitting in a hard-backed chair,
and I am looking out the window onto
the sound-asleep street below,
and a steady rain has turned into
an on-again-off-again affair,
and all I can say, dear Beth, is when you said—
as many times as there are leaves
in a grove of linden trees—
that you would wait for me,
I never once doubted that you would.

But why would you wait
so many years,
so many long and lonely years,
when doctors advised you
that I could sleep into eternity?
And why would you persevere
in coming to visit me
and hold my hand
and talk to me
when I was responsive as a log?

Perhaps it was in hopes
of salvaging something from that war:
if not your brother, Dominick,
then maybe me.

WAR WOUNDS

use this in
article?
or a -
pg it!

I wrote the U.S. Government
and asked them why they will not

award me the Purple Heart
for going insane in Vietnam.

Why isn't it a wound, I asked,
worthy of the Purple Heart

unless an arm or leg
or a chunk of a face or a hunk

of neck or back
gets blown away

by something like
a Chinese communist grenade

or a Russian artillery shell?
Why isn't it a wound, I asked,

worthy of the Purple Heart
when a mind is cut down

by nearly a year of things
inside a combat zone

like seeing seven men
out of nine in your squad

perish in a skirmish,
like trekking through triple-canopy jungle

lunging with leeches and mobs of mosquitoes,
like humping the boonies in clouds of burnt dust,

like holding dying comrades in your arms
then bodybagging them,

like tripping over ranges of ripsaw mountains,
like dragging Cong corpses into piles

then shooting their wounded,
like sloshing through monsoons in boot-sucking muck,

bathing hardly ever, never
sleeping soundly,

living on nothing but C-rations,
living in fear of the incoming mortars and rockets,

living in terror of land mines and booby traps
each step you take,

sweating every second when the next sniper
will have you in his sights,

till either your tour time or
your luck runs out?

The U.S. Government wrote me back
and said they were not awarding me

the Purple Heart
because my wound,

my type of wound,
did not draw blood.

QUIET CITY

*After an orchestral piece
of the same name
by Aaron Copland*

A sultry summer night too hot to sleep.
Unsticking myself from the bedsheet
as from a piece of Saran Wrap,
I slip on Nike shorts,
a pair of sandals
some apostle might have worn,
pop open a sweating can of Nesbitt's orange,
negotiate five rickety flights of stairs,
and exiting the rooming house
like a cat shooed out for the night,
I sally into the old West Side.

The city
quiet as someone
against whose face is pressed
a handkerchief
steeped in chloroform.

I glide along
like a skater on ice,
cross Wentworth, Otis, State
and Fillmore Streets, turn south
on Brewster Avenue . . .

overhead,
circling the streetlamps,
moths
like silent songbirds

in cages of light;
whatever breeze
U-turned by windbreaks of buildings;
whatever people
chased by the heat
like desert creatures
into the burrows of their abodes—

the heat,
the humid heat
reminding me of Vietnam,
expecting any moment to find myself
sloshing through rice paddies near Dak To,
or slogging with rucksack, M-16,
grenades and ammo belt
those misty valleys forty miles
northwest of Saigon,
or slumping against some termite mound
eating C-rations in Thoung Duc,
or diving into a thicket of bamboo
or elephant grass
dodging the sniper fire of Viet Cong
everywhere.

The city
quiet as an auditorium
of people joined
in a moment of silent prayer.

Six months home now
and still a thorn
in my thoughts is the day
my plane touched down

Home Coming

at Minneapolis-St. Paul International:
no friends,
no family
with "Welcome Home, Eugene"
balloons and banners;
no presidential envoy
to pin whatever on my chest
in recognition of
the twenty years yanked out
of my life like a tooth
(and a perfectly good tooth at that),
or to award me with
the Purple Heart
for the inoperable shard of shrapnel
embedded in my mind;
no ticker-tape parade
with marching band and majorette—
and yet, what government
in its right mind
would want to promenade
down Mainstreet, U.S.A.
for all the world to see
and listen to
some nut from Nam.

The city
quiet
as if the prairie were
reclaiming it.

Six months home now
and maybe it's for the best
I've yet to run into

some friend from before the Nam,
for if I did, as surely as
it's fish that swim and stones that don't,
he'd ask about the twenty years
since he last saw me and Dominick
in concert at Northrop Auditorium,
and after updating him
about the war,
about its sad side effects,
he'd either begin to weep,
or go and sit
until it closed
in some small bar.

The city,
like a child
exhausted by the day's adventures,
sleeps.

Six months home now
and still no friends,
six months home now
and only day labor,
twenty years
and I can't recognize
the city I grew up in . . .
and turning east on Robert Street,
I head into downtown St. Paul.

Arcing the Mississippi,
a suspension bridge;
the river reflecting the city's lights,

as if all the stars in the universe
were glittering beneath me—
a world turned upside down.

I clamber up the superstructure,
perch in a crow's nest of girders,
gaze at the city
outspread outrageously
as if some epic motion picture:

UNIVERSAL STUDIOS
presents

THE CITY

Cast of Millions

PRODUCER AND DIRECTOR
Cecil B. De Mille

STARS AND CO-STARS
Famous People

SUPPORTING CAST
Celebrities

MAKE-UP ARTISTS
Big Names

COSTUME
AND SET DESIGN
Oscar Winners

While I
am just an extra,
paid a pittance
for a bit part
in this spectacular—

my face is either seen
as something just outside
the camera's range,
always in the distance,
always out-of-focus,
or else as just another face
in a crowd scene;

my only lines are grunts
and mutters coming from
some warehouse or factory;

my name is never
listed in the credits.

And every day
the city pages overflow
with "Personals" advertisements:

people,
in a city of millions,
advertise for people;

people—
the city cursed
with a plague of people—
advertise for people;

people—
millions massed like armies,
as if the city were abutting borders
of warring countries—
advertise for people,
as if they've seen no signs
of humankind for years;

people—
millions nose to nose,
tramping each other's toes—
advertise for people,
each ad
as if a desperate note
that's folded, stuffed
into a bottle, corked
and set afloat
amidst a sea of people;

people—
millions moving always moving
on conveyor belts of streets and sidewalks,
as if the city were some giant factory
that only manufactured
people—
advertise for people,
each one alone
and lost
as if the city were some vast
bewildering wilderness.

I shinny down
to the foot of the bridge

where I see in full bloom
a night-blooming moonflower
that only blooms
when the night is the darkest,
when the city's the quietest.

I drain the Nesbitt's orange
and toss the can into a trash barrel bannered with:

Don't Be A Litter Critter

and cross Waconia Street
against the light.

This morning I looked out
the window in my room:
the buses packed with people;
the steady stream of cars and cabs;
the high rises
like giant stomachs
disgorging their contents of people;
mothers with babies in strollers;
black-and-white squad cars cruising by;
people mailing bills and letters;
U-haul trucks rumbling through traffic;
lovers sauntering past,
some with an arm around
each other's waist,
some with a hand inside
each other's back pocket;
people shopping for odds-and-ends groceries
at the corner Tom Thumb;
children with schoolbooks—

everyone going somewhere,
everyone with a purpose,
and all I can do is watch
like a bird with a broken wing.

As day is unaware
that night is creeping up on it
until too late,
so I am overtaken by
a sound
as much a part of the night
as dark itself,
a sound materializing from
the rooftop of some tenement,
the sound of an English horn.
With each step I take,
the sound takes a step of equal length.
And so we walk the city streets,
just I
and my new-found, albeit abstract,
friend.
Strange, how it seems less
the sound of an English horn
and more like someone's private thoughts
made audible.
And what is it he thinks?
He thinks of being anyone at all
except himself.
And now I try
but find I cannot hum
the melody he plays
any more than I could hum
the sound of someone weeping.

Across the cloudless sky,
heat lightning,
lightning unaccompanied by thunder.

Quiet,
storming over the city,
dripping off power lines
like sweat from fingertips,
flowing down alleys like lava,
pooling here in dips
where roots of trees heaved up
concrete blocks of sidewalks,
there in dents
on trashcan covers.

Quiet,
torrents of quiet,
storming over the city,
gushing off gutters
like waterfalls,
swamping the side streets
as if burst hydrants,
flooding the freeways
like ruptured reservoirs,
surging through tunnels like breakers,
making the pennants strung circus-like
around a used-car dealership
as silent as sails in dead calm.

Quiet,
a deluge of quiet,
storming over the city,
rising up the sides

of houses and buildings,
seeping under sills and jambs,
rising over the roof of Tom Thumb,
rising over the tops of tenements
stilling the English horn,
rising over the highest floors of high rises,
over the cables and girders of bridges,
over the summits of skyscrapers,
leveling every sound in its path
like a tidal wave,
burying the city beneath
an ocean of quiet.

And I,
as solitary a figure as
the shadow of a single cloud,
drift through the ruins,
as if I were the city's
sole
survivor.

ICE CREAM CONES, BALLOONS & CHILDREN

1.

It isn't every day
that a man goes to war,
nor is it every day
that a man goes insane.

2.

Aside from breathing,
the only thing
distinguished me
from someone
dead
was that I
smiled.

3.

The last thing I remember
before I went insane
was Eddie strolling back into camp
wearing a necklace made of human ears,
then everything faded into black,
as if I had crawled into a cave
deeper and deeper
till I could see
nothing but darkness,
till I could hear
nothing but silence.

And maybe in the way
that someone who is sentenced to
a term of time
in solitary confinement will
out of a kind of desperate loneliness
make a friend of a mouse,
to keep me company
my mind
created an image *an image*
as soothing as salve on sunburn,
an image of children.

4.

Each of the children held
in one hand
an ice cream cone
with double, even triple scoops
heaped high
on sugar cones
in simple flavors
like vanilla & chocolate & strawberry,
while in the other hand
each held balloons
in simple colors
like red & blue & green
that floated gaily overhead
like giant M&M's.

Nor was there anyone,
except the children,
nor anything at all
to clutter the landscape,
not even sky,

for if there were sky,
there could be clouds,
& clouds could darken into rain
or blacken into frightening storms—
so pure & simple was
the image,
so purely & simply happy were
the children,
they made me smile.

5.

A medical contingent flew me from Vietnam
stateside to a veterans hospital.
The children tagged along.

At first, the doctors felt confident
that they could remove the smile
as easily as if the smile

were painted on
like the smile on the face of a clown.
The smile thought otherwise,

for when the doctors injected me
with barrelsful
of lithium and Thorazine,

the smile just thumbed its nose;
and when they attempted
experimental drugs,

the smile just laughed at them;
and even when they administered
electroshock therapy

in dosages powerful enough
to flicker a city's lights,
the smile just shrugged it off like dust.

The doctors decided, over time,
that it was best
to simply let me be,

decided that the smile
they thought was painted on
was cast in bronze.

6.

If only the doctors,
if only my family
had known I wasn't suffering,
had known I was not alone
but had for company
the children
who never for a moment
ever left my side.

7.

And when the years of insanity
piled up like mountain snow,
what was it finally made me creep
closer and closer
to the mouth of the cave
and let me see,
instead of darkness,
light,
and let me hear,

instead of silence,
sound—
what was it finally made me say,
it's time,
and cut the cord
connecting me to Vietnam
and let me start breathing on my own?

8.

One day
the children
of whom I'd grown so fond
danced up to me
took both my hands in theirs
and started running,
ran and ran until
we stood outside the dream
and then I saw a bright
an almost blinding
light
and then I felt a familiar warmth—
it was the sun
and sitting beside me was a nurse
and trilling on a tree branch
a red-winged blackbird
and then I looked around
but the children were gone . . .

Some Can't Remember, Some Can't Forget

He walks in backwards every morning
fifty years in time,
olive drab
and government issued:

field cap, blocked;
hair short as stubble-beard;
face, battle-lean;
neck chain with dog tags;
fatigues starched stiff
as a week of death;
combat boots spit-shined mirror-black;
a hulk of field coat;
a hump of backpack.

If 1944 and tented battlefields
midst wild gardenias and biting jungles
of the Solomon Islands,
with every soldier,
with every clump of brushwood,
he'd blend in
perfectly.
But it's suburban Minneapolis,
and it's a chrome-plated carpeted workout room
appareled in designer warm-up suits
and name-brand tennis shoes,
the year is 1994,
and he is as out-of-place
as a barge in a creek.

He doffs his backpack and field coat.
He hoists a thirty-five-pound barbell overhead
as if a loaded rifle,
wades chest-deep through swamps.
He takes a towel and waltzes with it,
dodging a hailstorm of bullets;
then writes this moment into history
with a sidearm lob of the towel that destroys
a nest of enemy machine guns and artillery
inside the wastepaper basket.
He bellies up and bellies over
blasted walls of high-bar,
then crouches panther-deep and springs
up judo-wise and shadow-chops
at foreign throats and terrible faces.

Though he's been coming here for years,
all that's known of him
is every morning he appears,
is every morning when he's done,
he marches westward on Excelsior Boulevard
in quick time,
a-hundred-twenty steps a minute,
hands cupped, thumbs pointed down,

a-hundred-twenty steps a minute
everywhere he goes,
everywhere he goes
impaled to fifty years ago.

THE WALL

Dominick never made it home,
not even dead,
I think while walking through
the Vietnam Memorial
in Washington, D.C.

The day is just a child yet,
and snow is falling lightly,
and as I walk along the long
black-granite wall,
I pause, every now and then,

to look at the visitors:
all touch the wall,
all weep;
to look at some of the offerings
that comrades, friends and families have placed

at the foot of the wall:
a small American flag beside
a high-school graduation picture,
a Purple Heart pinned to the breast
of a neatly folded jungle uniform,

a stethoscope,
a note to Freddie from Diane,
a letter signed, love, Mom and Dad.
And as I scan
the nearly sixty-thousand names

of dead and missing,
of lives cut short
as day by an eclipse,
I hear a voice
resonating through the Memorial

as if a concert hall,
a voice
singing the lament
Vesti la giubba
from Leoncavallo's *Pagliacci*

and there, engraved on the granite wall,
I see his name.
I say, Hello,
hello, old friend,
and place my hands against the wall,

against his name,
and suddenly I am whiplashed back in time—
sun high overhead,
rice paddies everywhere,
our squad, two miles

from the Cambodian border,
is setting up an ambush,
when Dom goes down,
an arrow out both sides his neck,
a booby trap some guerrilla rigged,

and I am holding him,
and I am crying out
Medic! Medic!
who buries in his thigh
a syringeful of morphine,

and Dom is trying to talk to me
but all I hear
is the bubbling of his breath in his blood;
and after a minute, maybe two,
of timelessness,

the bubbling stops.
As Cecil and Punky ease Dominick
away from me,
Rudolpho radios for a medevac
while Paulson pops a smoke grenade

to mark the landing zone.
When Dom is loaded into the bird,
I watch
the dust swirling, the weeds waving
as it lifts off,

watch it veering over nameless hills,
watch it fading in the Asian haze,
watch the red tracer trails
fired from a VC .50-caliber machine gun
riddle the chopper,

watch as it explodes,
burns midair,
killing everyone on board,
killing Dominick again.
And it is now, once more, not then,

and with my hands still pressed
against the wall,
against his name,
I leave as an offering,
at the foot of the wall where I stand,

a vow of non-violence.

PART THREE:

New World

CONFESSIONS OF A MASS MURDERER
AND HIS REDEMPTION, OR,
SINCE VIETNAM

1.

I've left the battlefields behind,
I've laid my weapons down.
No difference anymore to me
the marshes along the Mekong Delta,
the mountainous jungles near Khe Sanh
where humans hunted down humans;

the lakes of Minnesota,
the woodlands of Idaho
where fish and deer are hunted down,
all battlefields to me now.
No difference anymore to me
an M-16, a BB gun,

a land mine, a fish hook,
all weapons to me now.
Call me
coward,
call me
bleeding heart,

say I'm inane,
say still insane,
but those who do,
didn't do what I did,
didn't see what I saw,
didn't have to

kill
for nearly a year inside
a combat zone
till I had neither the stomach nor the heart
for killing anymore,
for killing anything anymore.

2.

Wherever our unit marched,
from the swamplands in the south of Vietnam
to the mountainous jungles in the north,
were people,
and where there were people,
were cats and dogs,
were pigs and goats,
were chickens and water buffalo;

and other living things as well
were in the soil
where cities of little life forms lived
in every cubic yard;
were in the rivers, canals and streams
like fish and waterfowl;
were in the trees
like monkeys, birds and squirrels;

were in the air
like bats and bees and butterflies;
were everywhere
like jungle foliage

and ancient towering trees
when millions of tons of bombs,
when mortars, rockets and artillery
relentless as monsoonal rain,

when rifle and machine gun fire
as pitiless as a plague,
when oceans of Agent Orange
obliterated their lovely world,
obliterated them—
all casualties of the war,
all part of the body count—
how many because of me?

3.

In this new world of mine,
I've laid my weapons down,
a pile of weaponry
as high as a thousand-year-old redwood tree
and ten times wider than the tree is high:

the rifle and slingshot,
the hand grenades and spray cans of pesticide,
the bomber and boomerang,
the M-16, harpoon and fishing lures,
the missiles and bug-zappers,
the sticks and stones,
the mousetrap and rattrap and rod and reel,
the battleship and bayonet,
the ant poison and fly swatter,

the helicopter gunship and hunting bow,
the decoys and duck calls,
the fighter plane and fishing pole,
the flypaper and flame thrower,
the mortars and rockets,
the land mines and landing nets,
the ammo belts and bowie knife,
the tanks and artillery ,
the napalm bombs and high-explosive bombs,
the small-game gun and big-game gun,
the handgun and shotgun and blowgun and machine gun,
the barrels of Agent Orange.

Believe me,
no sooner would I march off to war again
than desecrate my parents' graves;
no sooner would I set a hook
in you, oh fish,
than someone happily swimming in a lake;
no sooner would I shoot
you from the skies, oh ducks, oh geese,
than angels if they dropped in;
no sooner would I overturn
the rock you live beneath, oh centipede,
than bulldoze my neighbor's home—
my only wish
with what few circles around the sun
remain for me
is to live in peace,
to walk through life

without life ever knowing that I walked through,
my voice no louder than
the heartbeat of a hummingbird,
my touch no rougher than
the light of a single star,
my footfall no heavier than
a speck of dust settling on a leaf,
for isn't there pain enough in life
without my compounding it,
and doesn't death come soon enough
without my making it sooner yet.

And if you still harbor any doubts
whether today,
or in the coming weeks or months,
I may revert,
then come, come closer to
the pile of weaponry
and see with your own eyes
and feel with your own touch
the decades of disuse—
how rust as thick
as a bear's winter coat
has frozen the weapons each to each
like drops of water in a block of ice;
how grasses and wildflowers,
how saplings of oak and birch,
of spruce and maple are reforesting
the pile
that will, in time,

dissolve into the earth,
into the air
as if it never was
and never should have been.

4.

Oh strangers and passersby,
let us become neighborly.

And you there, you with the lovely voice,
yes, you, oh crow,
come sit upon my shoulder for a spell
and sing a song for me.
Doesn't the symphony of life
have need for a percussion section, too?

And when you die, oh cow,
your bones collapsing under the weight of years,
I'll bury you,
I'll place a marker beside your grave
along with a nosegay of clover,
I'll say a prayer for you,
I'll weep for you.

And you, oh mosquito,
how tired and thirsty you must be
zinging through the hot summer nights.
Come rest upon my arm;
come quench your thirst,

for there is more than enough for both of us.
It isn't a fault of yours
the stream beside which you need to kneel,
from which you need to drink,
runs red inside of me.

And you, oh brother/sister worm,
come over by my side,
for soon you will make a meal of me,
and when you do,
I hope you find me sweet.

ACKNOWLEDGMENTS

Grateful acknowledgment is made to the publications in which the following poems first appeared:

A View from the Loft: "Some Can't Remember, Some Can't Forget"
Winning Writers: "Survival Manual for Vietnam"

The author extends heartfelt thanks to the Loft Literary Center in Minneapolis, Minnesota, for offering the classes and workshops where he first learned the craft of poetry; and to Deborah Keenan, John Minczeski, Michael Moos, and Jay White, the teachers without whom this book would have never been possible.

Special thanks is also extended to the competitions, sponsored by the Loft Literary Center, in which he was an award winner: The Loft Mentor Series, supported by a grant from the Jerome Foundation, and to Tim O'Brien, Maxine Kumin, Donald Justice, Etheridge Knight, and Toni Cade Bambara, the mentors with whom he studied over the course of a year. The International Residency Competition, supported by a grant from the McKnight Foundation, and to James Fenton with whom he studied for one month.

Most of all, the author wishes to acknowledge Gail, his wife, for her endless love and constant support.